The Poetry of Earth

The Poetry of Earth

Roger Roloff

illustrations by Ilka List

The Rhodora Press

The Rhodora Press
22 Hummel Road
New Paltz, N. Y. 12561

Front cover: a path to cranberries in the Shongum Mountains
Back cover (for the dedicatees): a well-matched pair of pink lady's-slippers

ISBN 0-9665367-1-1

Dedicated with love to my mother,
Margie Roloff, and to the memory
of my father, Raymond Roloff—
first and treasured readers

Contents

Author's Note

Certain geographical names and local expressions in this book place some poems in New York's Ulster or Greene Counties. The word "Shongum," used for example in "A Rattler Speaks Its Mind," is an authentic, two-syllable form of "Shawangunk" which neatly combines both spelling and pronunciation. Thus "Shongum grits," as used in "The Climber," indicate the quartzite crown rocks as they are locally called, whereas geologists refer to these hard, very old stones atop the Shawangunk Mountains as Shawangunk conglomerate rocks. "The Walking Stick" contains the old Indian word "Peekamoose" (one of several spellings), which denotes Peekamoose Mountain, at 3843 feet one of the taller Catskill summits. The "Doubletop" mentioned in "The Old Romancer" is another notable Catskill peak, slightly higher at 3860 feet. Lastly, the term "bluestone," which appears in "Berrycraft" and elsewhere, is what stonemasons call the sandstone strata found in the Catskill Mountains.

The Poetry of Earth

The Maples in a Drought Year

On such a cloudless day it seemed a crime
to dig through clay and stare at more post-holes,
and so to ease sore muscles at lunchtime
I walked and freed my eyes on pasture knolls.

The slow autumnal fire was at its height,
and gold contended with all shades of red
to dance, then rest awhile in warmer light.
From my stone seat I wondered what had fed
this maple blaze in summer, when the drought
that seared its way into each creature's mind
had dared to blacken all ere it was out.
I wandered in those lovely woods to find
the secret there, but only saw a coat
of many colors, partly dropped to earth
and rustling underfoot—October's note
that gives the hues above a dearer worth.
Somehow from long-parched land and scorching sky
the trees had earned a living and, from edges
of fields below to distant mountain ledges,
still cast a glow to measure Autumn by.

No post-holes lured me back to work that day.
Instead I sat upon a hilltop stone
and gazed at fiery boughs till sundown-gray
doused every flame. And I was not alone.

A Wild Grape Harvest

A thick, brown rope hangs from a massive oak.
I've never tried to climb it, but my eyes
race up it in the fall when, if it broke
tree-high, fox grapes would rain a sweet surprise.

They haven't yet, I see, but every time
I stare at fragrant clusters waiting there,
I wonder why birds pass, as if bird-lime
and not ripe grapes were dangling in the air.

A fox won't get them either, nor will I
stay longer than to shake my head once more,
then turn to lower vines I can't ignore
along a spicebush row that meets the sky
at just my height—and as in years before
will match, I'd bet, the vintage left up high.

Space Travel

Of course we're speeding through space now, and will
as long as our Earth-ship can carry us,
but modern Marco Polos scoff at that.
"Escape the gravity of this old sphere,"
they say, "and get a higher view of things."
With luck they come down safely, lofty dreams
betrayed by stammered words of homesick boys:
"The Earth has never looked so beautiful."
Up there they learn that cares of flesh and blood
lack weight—what any telescope makes plain,
or even two old naked eyes confirm.
Yet for the price of shoes and daily walks
those men could probe in depth the only space
that's missing in a heavenful of stars.
Just here sweetfern thrusts its spicy perfume
up an ambushed nose, fat blueberries drench
a greedy tongue, new columbines leap out
from shalebank eyries, clustered locust thorns
dare all tree-huggers. Distant Capricorn
will never hear a real goat bleat or know
the prairie warbler's scales from towhee trills,
but we can eavesdrop on the ageless blend
of Earthly voices in their seasons and ours.
And who would not sing a pulsing descant
on this oldest, rarest, wildest choral song?

A Rattler Speaks Its Mind

Here comes that hunter with his dog again!
He daren't shoot partridge now, but he'll sure strain
my patience and his beady eyes too long,
hunting out of season. He knows it's wrong,
but I am not the one to tell him, for if he
sees me he'll blow me to eternity.
Where is that warden, then? On holiday
at best; at worst, too drunk to find his way.
And this is how the State keeps riff-raff out!
So I'll just have to hide until the lout
and his big mutt give up and go back home—
and that's not near, I'd say, since farmers roam
these woods when leaves and harvest-time are past,
and not when planting must be done, and fast.
I had in mind a sunbath on this rock—
to feel spring at long last—and not to shock
trespassers—as they wouldn't call themselves.
With luck they'll blunder past these Shongum shelves
and head down to the brook to search by it.
Yet if they see me, they should have the wit
to know that they're too big to be my prey.
"Live and let live," I sometimes hear them say;
but do they ever, with or without guns?
It seems to me that native fear outruns
sweet reason in these beasts 'most every time.
The meal I make of chipmunks is a crime
to them who kill for sport, but never mind
the fact that *all* I eat is what I find
and neither waste nor wound and leave behind.
I can't obey their laws: I was here first,
and long before they came to do their worst.
These masters of destruction cannot build

without selecting something to be killed.
Would you trust creatures who have always thought
their will is all, and Nature can be bought?
That's how the upstarts work; but they must learn
their arrogance and money cannot earn
good credit there, and that their lucky birth
assures no life apart from Mother Earth.
There's room for them, if they can mend their ways;
but if they can't, how few their squandered days!
I will not miss them, if they go alone
and quietly; yet if the seeds they've sown
in their downfall should doom the globe we've known,
that end will not have come because an Eve
was tempted by my kin and had to leave
the paradise in which I still believe.

Song before Sunrise

Alone, hidden in foggy gloom,
a voice whistles, chatters, and slides
spring music into my bedroom.
Heedless of darkness on all sides
the merry singer pipes his song
across the frozen fields and lanes
from which the echoes, while less strong,
sneak through the frosty windowpanes.
The tune won't scare an owl in wait,
and though it's never guaranteed
to best rivals or win a mate,
it fills an ancient, inborn need.
Perhaps I shall not ever see
this redbird chant his joyous tones;
but as he sings them fearlessly,
I feel the song deep in my bones.

On Wings of Song

Unlikely serenader, plump,
short-legged, that sounds as if his rump
and not long beak produced the note
that's never quite unstuck from throat
and nose, the woodcock sits and calls
with growing urgency, but stalls
just as a climax might have come.
For then he leaves a brushy home
below and beats his stubby wings
to fill the air with twitterings
that climb until he's just a speck
and I have surely strained my neck.
But when it seems about to break,
he plummets, strewing in his wake
a liquid warble that bluebirds
might envy—yes, no other words
suffice for what the woodcock's done.
Of course it isn't Mendelssohn,
but who'd expect one bird to sing
these songs—on, off, and with the wing?
I know I'm humbled every year
I see the homely bird and hear
his twilight courtship repertoire:
he breaks the mold of singing star
for good, here in the dimming light.
And he may practice half the night—
until he's got each song just right.

The Vista in the Old Days

Last May I met an artist as he drew
a scene I've watched grow green for many springs.
He said the white ridgeline seemed always new
yet unchanged, though sometimes he wished for wings
back to a quieter age less spoiled by man
to see the cliffs and valleys in that light.
"Old pictures help," I offered. "If you can,
take time to study them for their insight."
But like impatient tourists passing by
he pressed me for the history I might know.
So I began, "Those cliffs that charm your eye
were back then dark with lichens; only snow
could make them gleam a hundred years ago."
He voiced surprise, and then I told him why:
"The lichens fell when acid rains arrived
to stay, and stricken lakes lost all their fish.
As strange as it may seem, the white's contrived."
He hesitated briefly, but his wish
to know won out and, pointing toward the tower,
he guessed one must have stood since human times.
"This one's the last of four; the weather's power
soon leveled wooden frames in these harsh climes.
Although old stones built this memorial,
it's stood for not quite eighty years this fall."
His gaze slipped to the trees below. I spoke,
unprompted, yet there was no gentle way
to say, "The land gave up its trees to smoke
and timber: farmers had to make them pay
until cleared fields made pastures or bore crops.
In those days stone walls that the woods now hide
marched uphill right to where the cliffline drops;
the trees you see were farmsteads that have died.

Old clear-cut landscapes, far from being preserved,
are not, I think, what you came here to see."
—There is no place to dream; those lives, reserved
for ceaseless toil, do not set fancy free.—
This self-reproach I did not speak, but thought
as the young man's eyes then searched the ground before
his sandaled feet, his neck and jawline taut.
He breathed a troubled sigh, and I forbore
to name still other facts; yet when I sought
a lighter note, he smiled but drew no more.
That may have been the last I'll see of him.
This March a friend said he'd moved to Nepal
and worships Buddha now; it was no whim,
she claimed, but with a pang I guessed at all
he'd left unsaid. Of course it had been he
who asked about the local history;
so if I told the truth I could not spare
his fallacies. And though I might agree
he's in Nepal without a thought of me,
I've heard the vistas are more stable there.

Ditch Flowers

It was a bluestone bluff, I think,
that brought me towards a facing brink—
a short way off across a gap
of trees, according to my map.
I must have entertained a hope
that on the cliff or nearby slope
I'd spy, with luck, a falcon nest
or greater prize I hadn't guessed.
June smiled and sent me on my way
and even lined the ditch that lay
beside the rising path with blue
and pink forget-me-nots, which drew
my eye and draw my mind's eye now.
Yet soon the floral overflow
was bluer than the whitening sky;
and clouds, instead of rolling by,
clung fast to every bush and tree
and suddenly enveloped me.
An hour I climbed and thought the sun
would pierce the mists or make them run,
but thick air had grown thicker still.
And so I trudged back down the hill,
abandoning the fog-stalled search
for one glimpse of a rock-walled perch.
The hike, I sighed, had come to naught,
when just then like a counter-thought
I met again clear, thinner air
and ditch flowers waiting for me there—
a drift of colors to complete
the sky's surprise, but at my feet.

Those flowers I never can forget.
As for the climb—I do not yet
remember why I sought the view
the day first promised, then withdrew;
but though it veiled that lofty bluff,
what it revealed was quite enough.

The Climber

What earthly good it was he couldn't say,
at least right off. But climbing suited him—
of that he was convinced, as he stared long
in early light toward pink rock turning white.
It tested flesh and blood in ways he liked:
the jagged edges, cracks, and crevices
he used to grip a sheer wall like a fly;
the dangers met and mastered, face to face
and each in turn; the plan to know *this* slope,
to meet *this* mountain on its own hard terms.
The rocks grabbed him as much as he clutched them,
and he gave up on scoffers who just joked
and pointed to the blue-blazed footpath up—
as though to skim the *Odyssey*'s Cliff Notes
meant tackling Homer's classic tale in Greek.
Of course the view on top drew everyone,
but what most missed the climber knew first-hand:
views up and down, around and through the rocks
that made his way of getting there the goal.
Close scrapes were part of that: the ledge he groped
that hid a copperhead, the flying bits
of Shongum grits he'd dodged, the time he fell
and dangled when the anchored rope had held.
And yet he still preferred free-climbing, gripped
by nothing but his own two hands and feet.
He found routes even better climbers missed
and would not take their limits as his own.
The strangest thing was that he didn't have
to climb at all—and yet he knew he did.
The cliffs he'd scale he first grasped in deep dreams—
bare-handed like another man who makes
his measured way to new-found mountaintops.

An Errant Song Sparrow

At first I thought the bird's dread foe
was but himself, caught by the glass
that matched his smallest move; but no,
his eye looked deeper with each pass.

And then he sang—and how he sang!—
to something on the sunlit sill
that seemed to hear his sweet harangue,
and yet sat motionless and still.

A sparrow made of glass that glowed
and sparkled in the morning sun
inspired the song that overflowed
and would a lesser mate have won.

The glass perfection on display
could never nest in any tree,
but still the singer piped his lay
to it in true idolatry.

That graven image, could it speak,
might well have warned: "Fool! sing your song
to fleeting, feathered love; don't seek
my fixed, mute form, though it last long.

"For all that flutters, flies, and sings
escapes a glass bird's perfect death
to know the joys and tears of things.
Deceiving glass can draw no breath."

Its power to trick is potent, though;
for even now the bird is singing fast
to stir his goddess here below.
He will not know such miracles are past.

New Nature

It's fair to say that beavers have no choice.
By Nature doomed to gnaw, they must destroy
young trees to thrive: to know that needs no brains.
Are they house-proud or smug with dams they build?
I cannot tell, yet they must know the cost
is worth their goal: to stand the test of time.

A clever man, indeed, might spend some time
to chew on goals and means apart from choice,
like beavers making livings—hang the cost.
Yet there it lies: shore saplings all destroyed
to make the brook a new-dammed pond, to build
the moat that stymies fox and coyote brains.

It must be plain to all but feeblest brains
that beavers use the Earth to stretch their time
on it. So must all life. Yet what they build
may seem to human heads the crueler choice
for aspens, grouse, box turtles: some destroyed,
some forced to scrape by at a dearer cost.

But miles of houses, endless concrete cost
the Earth a sum unknown to beaver brains.
If subtler ones slow-cooking it destroy,
as surely as split atoms may, life's time
by chance, then time and chance die with that choice.
Is this the barren rock we'd dare to build?

The Nature that we know could never build
itself anew if we exact that cost.
For a murdered world is no beaver's choice;
far greedier minds are needed. But such brains
are young and may not stand the test of time,
like cancer with the victim it destroys.

Perhaps old Nature will herself destroy,
wolflike, our rival ways. Or we could build
upon her, not unmake: there is yet time.
Perhaps we'll find that our new Nature costs
a world too much, and train the restless brains
before we have Earth without any choice.

What beavers can destroy has measured costs
for what they build. We cannot claim our brains
lack time to mend dire ways: we have that choice.

The Single Larch

The woods road tripped me up, and on sore knees
I saw through wincing eyes a strange, new weed.
How'd mulleins, thistles, burdock, brambles breed
small, golden-needled arms that wave like trees?
And then I knew. Somehow a lucky breeze
or passing bird or beast had dropped a seed
from larches far away. I'd had to bleed
to find that truth, but felt its pain soon ease.

Two years I'd berried past the seedling larch,
then missed it once more on each homeward march!
I chuckled at how Nature jolts our wits
in unguessed ways, mysterious and weird.
And yet, here these old tricks would fall to bits
if, years ago, the road had not been cleared.

Headwaters

The nameless stream long fed a waking dream:
to trace its scrawl from ribboned waterfall
to where the pen retracts beyond my ken.
I'd seen the brook break glassy ice in March
and sought its cooling waters in July
but had not found in that untraveled clove
the unmarked source that rocks and treetops hid.
I judged that April's thunderstorms might leave
a brawling echo there and was not wrong:
the roar that pounded through the gorge reached me
a half-mile sooner than I scaled a perch
to scan the broad, bright foam through naked boughs
of duller poplar, oak, and maple crowns.
Up to the distant crag the water seemed
to climb, and drew my eyes south till the sun
smote them; but I struck back by scrambling down
to meet the swollen brook on flooded banks.
A blind man could have trailed that lovely din.
On higher ground which logging roads once crossed
I found an upward path of rotting stumps,
now overgrown but here and there still marked
by slightest wheel-ruts, padded long by leaves.
I kept the stream in earshot as I curved
through hardwoods, mixed and ripe in second growth;
and when the water music ceased to match
the strength of treetop tunes that sighed above,
I swung back to the hemlock-shaded brook.
Its gurgling echoed by white arching rocks,
the slender stream soon split, and split again;
I tried each trickling route until I found
the right one, only dripping higher then.
The drips gave way to mossy, moistened rocks,

and then the moisture stopped. I peered around
and even felt the ground for one last seep,
but there was none. Somewhere beneath the shade
the looming crag threw down and under all
the shale and quartzite of its half-bald head,
wreathed by pitch pine and mountain laurel fuzz,
there dwelled a secret, well-protected spring.
No one can know that hidden, inner source;
I simply thanked the mountain for its gift
and marked where its deep mystery begins
with three cairns ringed around the first moist clue.
I've drunk these spring-fed waters all my life,
and they have never failed, but I do not
take them for granted—in dry years or wet.

The World That Got Away

I thought I'd never see one in these hills,
though I had searched so long in bogs, by kills.
But there it stood, or posed, on spongy ground:
a yellow lady's-slipper, just then found
by May's warm light through swaying tulip boughs.
I blinked to make sure this was no daydream,
then saw a second flower across the stream,
and then a third; and yet another rose
like magic on the cushioned banks of green.
I did not want to doubt what I had seen
but blinked again. Again the flowers remained
and caught those soft spotlights the sun had trained.
I threw my head back then and laughed with glee—
if only she could share this sight with me!—
and, gazing upward, saw the canopy
of tulips blend with elms—huge, healthy, old.
I stopped my laugh, not needing to be told
that these great trees which—I saw quickly—lined
the stream were rare as any flowers I'd find.
I wondered how for years I'd missed the elms
and orchids—with a thrill that overwhelms
cool reason—and so up the slope I sped
to reach the ridge and see the land outspread.
Was this the hunters' clove I'd always known
and where such trees and rare blooms had not grown?
As breathlessly I scanned the land below,
it seemed at once to answer yes and no.
The hills and valleys, thickly clad for spring,
were there; yet if land-tailors, measuring
the verdant cloth, had planned a patchwork quilt,
not one square touched what Nature's threads had built.

Amazed and baffled and yet strangely pleased,
I sat to ponder this new vision—seized
by that wild calm the land alone possessed.
I sensed I was the only human guest
to see, to feel an ancient realm made new.
Who would have dreamed it ever could be true?
So, thinking of one other soul to share
a world of which our age seemed unaware,
I glanced up, smiling at what rustled there,
let fall my eyelids while the old tree spoke—
it was a chestnut, not a chestnut oak—
leaned back against the trunk, and then awoke.

Trespassersby

A slender gap in that stone wall
gave tired old John a thought:
to cut across the pasture's sprawl
and hope he'd not be caught.

A neighbor farmer owned the land—
a new one he'd not met—
but surely he would understand
his neighbors posed no threat

to idle, stony, private ground.
John peered this way and that,
felt sure no other person was around
and, tilting his straw hat,

began to lumber up the field.
At once he thought he heard
birdsong that from some brambles pealed,
then saw a lone redbird.

He liked its ringing, merry song
and, veering toward the thorns,
he whistled as he walked along,
reliving bright spring morns

when he'd returned the redbird's tune.
Thus rapt, he did not see
another bird which swooped in soon—
known for its mimicry

yet not, perhaps, for its warfare
against all feathered foes
or passersby who seemed to share
its multiflora rose.

This warrior bird then dove and struck
at singers—bird and man;
as trespassers they had no luck
if they stayed put or ran.

The cardinal could not repel
the mockingbird's attack,
and in retreat some feathers fell
from battered wings and back.

Poor John fared worse, since he was sure
no *bird* could block his way;
he charged, but slipped on cow manure,
his hat squashed where he lay.

Yet as he rose, he could not clean
himself before the bird
chased him downhill, where he had been;
he felt and looked absurd.

That was the end of his trespass;
he took the long route home.
The redbird now sang for his lass
where both might safely come

to roost or build a nest for chicks.
As for old John, he learned
his lesson late, but those rough licks
were in his memory burned.

The mockingbird beat back all comers
till nestlings safely flew;
I've known good wardens in my summers,
but that bird tops those few.

How do I know all this? you ask.
Well, now: my barn's a glance
northward, where at some hayloft task
I worked; and so by chance

I saw John's rise and fight and fall,
yet didn't mind a bit
his harmless shortcut through my wall.
A bird might throw a fit

and think its claim is absolute,
but owners come and go.
And if I really gave a hoot
I'd mend the wall just so

each neighbor knew where he should walk,
and where he'd see a cow.
That's how old, fussy owners talk;
I disagree—for now.

The Preferred Habitat

Three hours before a winter dawn, how far
we drove to pristine woods that barred owls haunt—
so we were told—and more folks came by car

to join the hushed search, or at least to flaunt
their gear and brag in *sotto voce* tones.
Perhaps the owls caught this and, just to taunt

the bone-chilled experts, sat as still as stones.
Thus not one gliding form could we detect,
or muffled hoot amid the hemlock moans.

Dawn broke, and we, too weary to inspect
each branch, left the trees to those stealthy fowl.
Back in home woods, where we did not expect

the noon sun to betray a perched barred owl,
it did. Nearby one hooted on the prowl.

Juneberrying

It was a cedar-bird
that landed just head-high
on shadbush I'd paused by
one June the twenty-third.
He quickly plucked a berry
and ate it while I stared,
then plucked one more to carry
and flew, but where he fared
I could not follow long
with eyes or plodding feet.
And so I turned to eat
one berry from the throng
of red and purple fruit
that hung in dappled light,
then birdlike followed suit
and tried one more small bite.
The taste stirred memories
of finer cherries, hints
of almonds; and the breeze
caressed the forest tints
as I ate on, at ease.
I'd wandered out to test
the season's first blueberries,
but they had not possessed
that full ripeness which tarries
upon a grateful tongue:
they were ten days too young.
These Juneberries had shown
my palate such rare flavor
I'd otherwise not known
but for a bird's chance favor.

And though I was alone
and might have filled a pail,
I thought one guide who'd flown
yet taught what could not fail
to nourish me years hence
should have his recompense.
The cedar-bird I'd seen
did not return before
I left, and yet between
that day and this the more
Juneberries I pick and store,
the more he's come to mean.

The Old Romancer

They say the old romancer's dead at last—
that after all the tales he swore were true
he died quite peacefully at home in bed.
He would have loved the irony in that,
just as he'd often fool a bug-eyed crowd
which, from his voice and knowing manner, thought
he'd played in all the scenes he brought to life:
that was his art.

          When he was young and quick
he may have teased the rattlesnakes out West
with only canes or walking sticks until,
their rage and strength subdued, they slithered off.
Back here the cougar that he found and stalked
without a gun when he was forty-eight—
that stretched the truth, some thought, till one big cat,
long-tailed, was spotted slinking near a barn
not seven miles from town soon afterward.
I drew the line at one late polar trek,
though that gripped me when he recounted it
far more than films I saw before or since.
And so I cannot say when courtroom truth
merged with his subtle skill: he was that good.

Some things I knew he'd lived through he'd confide—
but haltingly—in private to a few.
For years he'd known a world shot up by war;
he dressed men's wounds and met their anxious eyes
with consolation—those whose gaze smiled back
and those who soon stared at oblivion.
Each day his sun shone through the dismal ward,
where evil shadows hovered, merciless,
as they enshrouded battlefields nearby.
But when the man-made thunder stopped at last,

he fell apart inside. Rebuilding that
made him a soldier for wild Nature's peace—
as when a healthy oak, surviving drought,
grows great and old, quietly adding rings.

Perhaps that's why, when burdened by a world
that Nature's only lately known, he'd walk
into the hills and cloves that human hands
have not disfigured. There he'd roam for days
or sometimes weeks, in weather fair or foul,
until he paused in his long dialogue
with birds and brooks and secret witness trees
where he had camped. He left reluctantly,
but brimming with new tales and seasoned thoughts.
Tumbling out, they matched dark but flashing eyes
and sometimes tripped his tongue; we shared a laugh
at mixed-up names of orchids which he feared
were gone for good but spied near limestone shelves.
He'd shake his head, then tell of a plane wreck
on Doubletop, slowly disappearing not
from human scavengers but in the jaws
of porcupines which got their salt that way.
And once he brought a kind of violet
that none of us could find in any book.

You won't find *him* there either, for the fame
that others blindly craved did not tempt him.
Mere print on paper—he left some behind—
could never translate how his voice-tones, face,
and hands spoke volumes in all earthly tongues.
What like a bard he bequeathed to the air—
the rare music he made alone from words—
has lodged itself deep in our memories.
Now he belongs forever to the earth
and air and rain that bore him, but the fire
that glowed in him shall not be seen again.

A Face Cord

I once was skeptical of such half-cords
and thought them tricks on rash, unwary buyers
who didn't grasp the small, plain woodlot-words
until too late, then swore they'd bought from liars.
Now I'm not sure. Last fall two cords of wood
lay like a heap of words in too-free verse
across the street; and buried in what should
have been just oak were popple, pine, and worse.

Next door a single well-stacked hardwood row,
air-dried all year, showed not a misplaced stick
from either side or solid end, down low
or higher up: that job was no cheap trick.

I'm glad the work's on view: that neighbor knew
he owned an honest eight by four by two.

The Walking Stick

Some years ago on Peekamoose I learned
that climbing down on three legs made the chore
less risky than on two just lately turned

to rubber but more bruisable and sore.
A slim ash-limb lay right beside the trail;
I grabbed it as cold rain began to pour

and used the pebbled path as streambed braille.
Although I had a long and soggy trip
back down, the weathered ash-stick did not fail

to keep me upright when my boots would slip;
for walking back, as I soon understood,
meant trusting that third leg and my firm grip.

Once home I looked at saplings in my wood
with different eyes, and searched within the grove
for straight, hard shafts whose smooth young bark felt good.

The hickory I chose from that green trove
I cut to match my height of six-feet-two—
and thus to grow my reach around, above,

below to double length in just a few
fleet movements, or a double strength to wield
at once if sudden need or danger grew.

And what I would not touch the staff could shield
me from: sharp thorns and poison ivy vines.
Yet, strangely and most often, I would yield

to rambles that stick even now combines
with mine, and find myself drawn up a slope
or down a clove's unusual designs.

The stick, it seemed, showed me the hidden scope
of any land, and pointed out—as if
a thought probed with it—signs or only hope

of here corydalis along a cliff,
there cranberries through veils of tall marsh grass,
swamp honeysuckle from the merest whiff.

In truth the staff led me where I might pass
but once what later I could not forget,
those secret lives hid by a mountain's mass.

And nearby trails hold wonders I've not met
as well; but with its daily, gentle prod
the staff and I will likely meet them yet.

One day—far off, I trust—the sturdy rod
and I will part; for good, hard hickory
will shine in use when my dust joins the sod.

May it serve then as it so long served me
and guide another wanderer to know
new paths in its well-seasoned company.

Yet till my steps have grown too weak or slow,
the tough-grained staff for my grip ready stands
to tap its steady rhythm as I go,
still polishing its bark with practiced hands.

A Sparrow's Fall

No breath of breeze, just the shimmer of heat
lay on some fallow land that plow and axe
had cleared long years ago for winter wheat,
not blooming steeplebush and wild yellow flax—
a summer home where sparrows combed the field.
Amid their foraging and lively talk
of crowded nests and food the land might yield,
they failed to see a small and stealthy hawk.

In an eye-blink it snatched an older bird
and fled before the unsuspecting flock
too late screamed its alarm. But no eye blurred
in mourning, nor did dazed survivors' shock
keep them—soon sure no other hawk might lurk
nearby—from quickly going back to work.

A Great Man's Centennial

Just he and I were there that day in June.
Such melody joined earth and sky! Mere words
could never match the white-throat's haunting tune,
his lifelong favorite of all songbirds.

The sparrow made me think again on what
I'd planned to read from, just for him: his book
on spring that many praised and yet forgot,
in spite of all the years of care he took.

Instead I studied woodland gifts that last—
his wise advice—strong-rooted laurel, pines,
forget-me-nots, shadbush, and columbines
his earth renewed, that at his side stood fast.
They'd long embrace, with their wild, shady mass,
his name carved in bluestone—misspelled, alas.

The Pasture Hickory

I never saw it when the thick, high crown
gave cows cool shelter during August droughts,
but only knew its fame from farmers' tales.
One told of how the sapling, spared by saws
that cleared some forty acres for the herd,
became a perch for falcons bred and trained
by a dairy-farmer's only son, half-blind.
Another claimed the grass wildfire that ate
that year's hay crop just licked the shaggy bark.
And then one stormy day a lightning bolt,
well-aimed, electrified the towering trunk
and threw three big limbs crackling to the earth.
(A hired girl saw this, and today her eyes
blaze white in fright when she remembers it.)
The battered hulk that guards the pasture now
gives pricey thoroughbreds its shrunken shade.
Last fall along with nuts it dropped a branch—
an old buck shedding antlers one more time—
and I dragged home a souvenir yule log.
That New Year's Eve with one matchstick I freed
the captured summer warmth of six score years,
then fried a hearthside breakfast with the coals.
The hickory, meanwhile, withstood a storm
that glazed its gray, gnarled skeleton in ice:
assaulted yet again by heaven's whim.
At dusk the old tree's frozen silhouette
looked barren as the grave; but by May's dawn
the buds had swollen, burst, and upthrust leaves
demanded of the sun another year.

Survival Is the Main Thing

Eggs that cunning, furtive mothers
lay in sparrows' nests, and others',
hatch not knowing that their siblings,
often smaller (like their nibblings),
are no sisters or true brothers.
Lucky cowbirds, far from grousing
over foster-care and -housing,
will survive, without complaining,
borrowed room and board and training.
If one meets his mother later,
can he even know or hate her?
Tribal instinct here is stronger—
many million years the longer—
than the moral codes that wrong her.
What some scorn as parasitic,
if they were more analytic,
slights the birds' sly, well-timed daring,
looks past awkward truth they're bearing:
Mother cowbirds' life-or-death tricks
long pre-date our tender ethics.
Furthermore, the outlook's fine
for cowbirds and their lengthy line,
though they're all foundlings by design.

A Tenant Farmer on the Owner

As long as anybody can recall
she's owned this land. She's watched her plantings come
and go and let her livestock freely range.
(She pays no mind to gates and fences, yet
her boundaries are clear to any creature
that has long survived her rigors and moods.)
She cut and dug the streambeds on her ground
all by herself and handles each one's flow.
A careless harvester, she builds her soil
with cover crops the seasons feed and weed.
And though her patience can outlast a glacier,
surprise is probably her oldest trick,
as time and again she creates new breeds
and hybrids in experimental plots.
She waves aside all theories, and tests
each new arrival in the long run she
invented and which I can only dream of.
To her I must appear preoccupied
with cultivating *some* of what I call
her useful wild beauties, yet in my work
I keep reminding her of all they mean.
She plays no favorites, of course, but if
she's in a listening mood, I'll seize this chance
to let her know how glad I am to be
her tenant for as long as she allows.

A Double Rainbow

The storm boiled up from week-long haze
that kept us in its sweaty grip.
Dark clouds had massed on several days
and thunder drummed, but not one drip
had moistened busy, sunburned hands
or touched ripe blueberries they picked.
This rain slid east toward fertile lands
below our mountain patch, then tricked
us quickly while our backs were turned
by throwing lightning bolts too near.
We fled to field-edge trees and learned
afresh an ancient, breathless fear
as maples swayed and leaves in terror
flashed white and chattered, blown out straight.
Whipped by sharp gusts, if we in error
had huddled here, it was too late
to run elsewhere. Too late indeed
for a tall black gum, made more black
by one white, deadly bolt that freed
its crown to lie among hardhack.
Not far away we cringed and watched
the wreckage smoke in driving rain.

Slowly the angry sky, still notched
by crackling, jagged fire, again
grew merely gray and passed the storm
to other mountains in the range.
Then through the clouds the vaulting form
of rainbow twins painted a change
we cheered aloud in our relief.
The valley farms, thus overarched,
seemed strangely blessed, as though their brief

encounter with the brute that marched
to fearsome drumbeats through our patch
had given them a teasing shower.

It was not so. A news dispatch
we read dwelled on a twister's power
and sudden chaos, farmhands dead.
A double rainbow spanned a crest
above the farms—one witness said—
some lucky woods and fields just west.

After Cranberrying

Leaves of heath have caught red fire;
crimson berries gave their best,
slow harvest, matching my desire.

Now the land, so richly dressed,
basks one last time in milder air,
sheds frosty dew, and waits for rest.

Hazy warmth I gladly share,
pausing to rub sore knees and thighs.
Too soon bushes will be bare,

whistling when gusts fall and rise.
Sitting here with harvest done,
I breathe deeply, close my eyes,

dream of fruits in next year's sun;
yet my foraging pursuits
these creeping plants will long outrun.

Lacking their perennial roots—
lured like mice or passing birds,
sowing seeds by picking fruits—

I may live, but just through words.
Some men think that this wild ground
serves their will like docile herds;

far older plants have always found
truth is the other way around.

Notice in Perpetuity

It marks a mountain trail on a dead tree:
"You pass at your own risk. This notice frees
the owner from all claims of injury
or harm." Or wasted words, too, if you please.

I passed the hand-carved sign with that light thought,
then plodded switchbacks on the long, steep grind.
Yet now and then the sign's old letters caught
at childhood memories rising in my mind.

Although this was my first climb here, I knew
but could not place that script from long ago.
By nightfall I gave up—however true
the feeling seemed. The most I'll likely know,
I mused about the sign in starlit cold,
is that it's based on others eons old.

Berrycraft

And if I tell you where the berries are,
then, Mrs. Newstead, would you walk that far?
I found them in the Shongums—that you know—
but would a map that shows just where to go
reveal too much if just one neighbor saw it?
Our secret's safer still if I don't draw it—
don't you agree?—and safe as safe can be
if I don't share it with a soul save me.
Don't get me wrong: I know you'd cross your heart
and promise to keep mum. That's not the part
that worries me. Let's say you find the patch.
If I know anything, you'll have to catch
yourself when neighbors see the ripe, black fruit.
They'll gently pry; you'll want to brag, and toot
your horn a bit, then blush and toot some more—
and suddenly your secret's out the door.
Oh no! you say; that's not the way I'd be!
How can you be so sure? Just look at me:
about to tell you, all for friendship's sake,
my secret in less time than it would take
to pick a pint—too cheap for friendship, eh?

Now here's a thought that in the end might weigh
much more in friendliness and berries, too.
I'll keep my secret, but I'll give a clue,
or sev'ral, leading to a patch for you.
Go see the woods roads first, especially those
the sun smiles on, where leafy arms don't close
above or keep square, thorny canes in shade.
Then look down at the road. If it is made
of shale—don't ask me why—the roots will thrive

so that you'll think the gravel bed's alive.
And bluestone's good as well; the main thing here
is that old, rocky roads bring brambles near.
Don't skip the ditch or banks. They channel rain
and often hide where berry-clumps have lain
until you find them. So a walking-stick
is handy there, to lift them as you pick
into a bucket on your belt, not prick
your fingers holding thorns while stooping low
to slip and drop black jewels off your toe.
That stick will grab steep hillsides, too, and hold
you firm while canes displaying their black gold
will meet one robber and be gently rolled.
And bramble tangles no one dares to touch
won't frighten your stout hickory stick that much;
you'll simply swing the canes back wide
and take your fill of clusters deep inside.
Sounds almost easy, eh? Well, don't forget—
unless you're working up a Catskill sweat—
our lower Shongum slopes grow three-leaved plants
whose touch will make you wish instead for ants.
It's poison ivy's itchy fire I mean,
so look sharp and remember where it's been.
Because it grows right where some berries sit,
remember, too, it scares away (to wit)
unwary folks who touch more than a bit.
That leaves the patch to you, aside from grouse
or turkeys or rare bears that roam and browse.
You'll see more scat than anything, but, still,
you might spy fur or feathers up a hill,
then watch them disappearing with a will.
Oh, yes—don't look for snakes. They'll look for you
and slither off—as if your steps yelled "Shoo!"

That doesn't mean your boots should hit the ground
before your eyes alertly look around.

And now I fear I've rattled on too long.
Not yet, you say? Well, ma'am, it would be wrong
if I left out one last, important thing.
You know those tunes that opera tenors sing—
the songs as beautiful as they are tough
to do until a person's trained enough?
To pick wild berries is a bit like that.
To figure out blackberries' habitat
rewards you more than packing out the goods:
if you know their home well, you know the woods.
And when you find a secret berry trove,
keep it that way, if only for the love
of berrycraft. The world will never lack
for berry-eaters, but, in losing track
of finders' arts, it slips a little back.
So, Mrs. Newstead, if a friend you've fed
asks where you found them, let him hear instead
some tips to feed himself, just as you learned.
Wild berries taste the best when they're well-earned.

Shelf Apples

How far the shiny fruit has come—
"Cross-Country Reds!" the label shouts,
as if they'd run here, or that some
new hybrid tops those hereabouts.

Yet either way the special breed,
I'm sure, will have to look the part
of Renoir's perfect fruit indeed
to grace a shelf or shopping cart.

To get to that exalted state
an apple needs the man-made shields
against so many mouths that wait
impatiently among the fields;

thus treatments for a worm or rust
are joined by sprays against the birds
but not the bees, by toxic dust
whose name runs on like ten long words.

Still other dangers like late frost
just when buds burst, or early drops
of half-ripe fruit—whole seasons lost—
can plague the hapless apple crops.

It is enough to test the nerves
of any clever man: to see
that harvest he by sweat deserves
fight being his commodity.

And if the crop escapes at last
each hazard on the farmer's land,
the coddled fruit he'll harvest fast
may blush in ripeness yet taste bland.

A single bite is all, in short,
we'll ever need to show ourselves
that apples of this shapely sort
are better decorating shelves.

I'm told the market won't allow
for blemished fruits, though they taste good;
the spotless kinds, at least for now,
must do, although it's understood:

Had Eve fed Adam one of these
while God just looked the other way—
more fond perhaps of birds and bees—
the serpent would have lost his prey.

To My Garden

When you say "beans," just as I taught,
remind me that what you have wrought
surpasses merely human thought.

When you but stammer "beans" to me,
help me regard them thankfully
for what I see and do not see.

And when you barely whisper "beans,"
give me a nudge behind the scenes
of fall to ponder what spring means.

Ghosts

I cannot see ghosts as they're advertised
in houses: there the only spooks I find
scurry with mouse feet, gnaw holes squirrel-sized,
show where raccoons have lately slept and dined.
More likely haunts are maps which, unrevised,
evoke a trace of stubborn memory
that lingers and, if closely scrutinized,
lives on in yesterdays that scholars see.

More lively spirits dance and sometimes sing
in storytellers' oral craft, and yet
the longest-living ghosts that I have met
survive and even thrive by conjuring
imaginative print that does not age
upon a single well-performing page.

The Problem Tree

My neighbor says he wants my dead elm down.
"Just wait," I tell him, but his peevish frown
shows me that he meant safely down, away
from his prized boxwood hedge and new rosebay.
He knows the bare and broken crown leans east
towards my berry patch, and at the least
I'll lose a maple when the big snag falls.
"That tree won't squash your chickweed or oak galls,"
I tease, but he just bristles and stalks off.
The gaunt elm's tall, yet it's not close enough
to harm my crabgrass right beside his hedge.
Just sixty years ago what's now his wedge
of ground grew trees that lived and died in peace.
Here first, they couldn't buy a deed or lease
to bar upstarts who seize the land like prey.

Since there's no court to give the trees their say,
a few of us may look past metes and bounds
and think, perhaps, of tiny peeping sounds
that led most years to this elm's oriole nest,
rocked wide by winds, and higher than I guessed.
When foot-long strips of bark peeled off and dropped,
woodpeckers of all beaks flew in and stopped
to drum awhile or carve a hole for ants.
One penthouse O, pecked deep by skill, by chance
was home to red-belly chicks, fledged last May.
And more birds found the barkless boughs each day:
from hawks to smallest wrens, the simplest way
to see and be seen was to land up there
and sing or preen or simply take the air.
I ought to know; I saw them all, as clear
as polished lenses let me, one rare year.

The crown is toppling now, and yet this week
a frosty, gray November turned less bleak
when crown-logs warmed and lit my hearth at night.
Their trademark scent and odd blue-yellow light
returned me to bonfires of boyhood, stoked
by brushpiles and weed-trees that hissed and smoked.
Though cross-grained elm is no one's cordwood tree,
why scorn well-seasoned limbs nearby and free?
I'll scavenge elm bones winter storms may fling
and dream of morels 'round the stump next spring;
but if the snag and woodpeckers' luck have stood,
an old high-rise will shelter one more brood.
Were half our parting gifts to Earth as good!

Cold Comfort

One golden eagle I can not forget—
perched on a crag I'd nearly scrambled by
in misty, raw November air, too wet
to walk in comfort through, worse yet to fly.

A white neck-patch upon the brownish gold
stood out, which with a closer, harder look
became a weasel skull, its deathly hold
still firm, although my strong field glasses shook.

The grisly battle medal this bird wore
had stirred down deep an older, unhealed wound.
I peered again at the skull's cold, grim mouth
and rued the griefs that few survivors bore.
In silence I hiked on; mists swirling 'round,
the eagle sailed off—flapping, gliding south.

Among the Ruins

In pathless upland woods I found a house
in ruins and some old hand tools within.
The only resident I saw, a mouse
that fled, could hardly care what they had been,
and hid behind the handle of a plane—
so it appeared, despite the years of rust
which dulled the unused blade where it had lain.
Nearby from a lone chestnut beam what must
have been a scale hung still, but now it weighed
a bird's nest, not scoopfuls of buckwheat flour.
Long idle are the minds and hands that made
such tools, in dust the measures of that hour.
The afterlife, it's safe to say, designed
some jobs those craftsmen didn't have in mind.

The Frozen Waterfall

Five years before in March I'd seen it first,
dropping hard, spiked hair from an icy beard
that melted underneath and quenched my thirst.
In truth it was the brook below I'd *heard*
that led my eyes zigzagging to the fall
which gleamed and sparkled when the sun took aim.
I clambered up the slope to see how tall
it was, this waterfall without a name.
Just ten feet high, the cascade could been seen
and heard, I found, due east a quarter-mile
across a nameless clove that lies between—
and that long view might any eye beguile.
My steps perhaps are slower now, and snows
December piled too deep have hid the way,
but presently the crystal sculpture glows
before me on the old year's shortest day.
The fall is just as I recall, except
the greater thickness of the beard, whose hair
drips water that the brook above has kept,
ice-dammed, for any creature passing there.
Mouth wide I crouch to catch the chilly drops
and feel the cold elixir thrill my tongue,
while overhead a busy birdlet hops
along a hemlock branch. He is too young
to know me from before, this chickadee
that pecks at seeds, then flies down to the brook
to drink quite near and, as it seems to me,
to sing hello and get a better look.
I tempt him with seeds from my pocket, tossed
trail-like to lead him gently to my hand.

He takes the bait and doesn't mind being lost
awhile in this small world—new-made, unplanned.
If he cannot surmise how I have found
myself in *his*, for him the why is clear
when he has eaten up the tiny mound
of seeds and flies off singing, full of cheer.
I kneel by the brook for a long, deep drink.
The stillness of the woods I drink in too,
and wonder what the clock-bound world will think
when, hours from now, I lumber into view.
I'll only say, "I saved the solstice day
to see a frozen waterfall and tame
a chickadee. I may have lost my way
in finding them, but that is why I came."

A Woodcutter's Prayer of Thanks

I thank the ancient power that brought me here
when January fills the woods with snow
and sends a pair of frosty days so clear
that sunlight scatters diamonds below,
for then my work with sharpened saw and axe
will let me build the old and careful way
full hardwood cords to join in measured stacks
the tinted silhouettes that close each day.

No less do I give thanks that when brief thaws
bind saws, and wedges more than axe-heads bore
through knotty cores, I still in sweat may pause
with one face cord; and give thanks even more

that on days dark and inhospitable
I cleave a stump I thought unsplittable.

A Winter Hawk

I sometimes see him mobbed by sniping crows
that now and then will risk a sudden peck
behind his back, there in the barren wreck
of snags. He tries to wait out these old foes,
for what he needs hides under still, deep snows;
but if he soars to flee, if not to check,
their taunts till he's a microscopic speck
high up, he'll come back to a roost he knows.

Left to himself he'll grasp a good perch tight,
until the merest hint of life stirs eyes
that burn holes in the groundling prey whose sight,
snow-blinded, may not let it recognize
the patient hunter diving for his prize,
his thought made real upon a field of white.

Winter Tulips

Like petals dropped below,
winged seeds from tulip boughs
I find beneath a row
of tall, straight trunks that house
what birds and squirrels hunt
aloft or on the ground
to overcome the want
that winter spreads around.
Though winds blow fierce and chill
and many petals fall,
though small mouths eat their fill,
no winter gets them all.
The spikes and rims of cones
remain to catch low rays
and glow with golden tones
amid the frozen days.
Like candelabra lit,
the sun-struck seed-cup flowers

will keep their gold and sit
to bathe in April showers.
In February cold
they lift my gaze as high
as heaven, and enfold
rapt thoughts as, by and by
in hushed, deep afterglow,
I turn slow steps toward home
and wander through the snow
into a starlit dome.

Arbutus Days

The green leaves peeked from snow
which fell so long ago,
it seemed, that tardy spring
would not be answering
gruff winter's wild north wind.
But these leaves paid no mind,
for there they were in spite
of all the frozen white
and even hikers' boots
that tore at stems and roots.
I dared not hope for flowers,
for in two sunless hours
I'd not yet seen a bird.
Still, something must have stirred
a single bumblebee
which, humming moodily,
flew near, then buzzed by me.
He lit on that green patch
I'd glimpsed, but what he'd catch
lay tucked beneath the green
where he soon probed, unseen.
In moments he flew off;
for now he'd had enough.
Yet I had not, and pried
for what he'd somehow spied,
then felt and saw and smelled
the tiny blooms that swelled
with fragrance, strong and sweet.
These flowers that other feet
had nearly crushed foretold
what she and I of old
had named Arbutus Days,
when all we sought were ways
and paths and trails that went

to that unrivalled scent.
So as I stood to go
I smiled at falling snow,
for what I'd sing that night
would fill her eyes with light:
"Old winter's on the run;
arbutus time's begun!"

Shadblow Time

The small white flowers of old adorned
a coffin when the frozen ground
at last had thawed, and those who mourned
might lay them on the burial mound.
So they have served, these early blooms
of humble shadbush, slender trees
whose vernal understory rooms
lure spring-starved eyes and hungry bees.
I seek them out in April sun
when warmer breezes dance with me,
and up streams shad so freely run
I half believe they spawned the tree
that bears their name. Shy bloodroot flowers
may quickly go and dead leaves hide
hepatica too many hours;
but when shadblow waves far and wide,
I see the white flags winter's spread
and know for sure the old man's dead.
Sweet resurrection's next, and soon
the snow-fed, gray-brown land will make
fresh green, from which many a tune
will swell with news: Earth is awake!

The Skeptic Bird

"Tut, tut," say high-pitched, nasal notes.
They don't come from romantic throats
or thoughts, but tellingly express
a prudent living made with less.
The courtship song, short and no better,
must turn one head, for its begetter—
so it seems—seldom lives alone.
The shy mates like the trees they've known
since flying from a knothole nest
and won't spend winter in Key West;
they tough it out through snow and sleet
and somehow find enough to eat.
The furrowed bark they spiral down
must hold a feast indeed; I own
I've never found a nuthatch gaunt.
That thrift and chiding call may taunt
the land-consuming human neighbors
to master modest, Earth-wise labors.
Yet even if the gibe rings true,
what skeptic takes the rosy view
(the nuthatch surely mocks it too)
that humankind believes a word-
like sound that's uttered by a bird
which sees life upside down? Absurd!

An Honored Guest Thinks
  before Speaking

This well-lit space is like a one-room school,
and I must try to teach all grades at once.
Will goosefoot focus middle-aging eyes
and hold them from sheer curiosity?
Might rowdy youngsters tumble to sweet bait
of mulberries and pick them in July?
Could white and balding heads think seriously
of spicing salads with some winter cress?
I can't be sure, but I expect surprise,
for people mirror Nature that way too.

I'm foraging for minds and wills, of course,
and they cannot be picked like trailside greens.
Perhaps I'll only scatter mustard seed;
but I won't cheat by *tilling* unclaimed ground,
since these folks—if they want to—have to learn
to reap where they have never sown or searched.
Some minds will close like bloodroot blooms at dusk
when one voice chills the air by asking how
to slip by poison ivy, snakes, and ticks.
And skeptics, like school troublemakers, doubt
that one man in November—I—could wrest
from Pennsylvania's woods and fields and streams
enough to make a week's wild living on,
and even gain two pounds while camping out.
"How would you do it, then?" I'll ask, and when
tongues tie or trip or halt, I'll lead lame thoughts
to our own ancient grandams and grandsires
and ask if we are somehow less than they.
"Oh, no!" the scoffers say, yet in their eyes

I spy an honest doubt, one that admits
of true wildcraft, forgotten for too long.
When teacher's pets must parrot gleaning tips
they cribbed perhaps from me, in flattery,
I'll thank them all, reminding them again
that in my text on foraging it says
to read the book of Nature—all of it—
so that the taste of mustard greens takes in
as well the creaking oak, the flicker's cry,
the brook that bathes marsh marigolds nearby.
If luck and wit have not deserted me,
then thoughtful questions—as, "When is enough?"—
will find deep balances in my reply:
Day-lilies or the blooms of violets
can feed a growling stomach and teach taste buds,
yet feasts for eyes may have a greater worth.
My aim in living is to cost the Earth
no more than it can bear or safely share,
to joy in that wild thrift from year to year.
Why ask for more from Nature, or expect
to rule a kingdom I cannot possess?

Did I speak that, or think it loudly now?
All eyes are on me, and a high-pitched voice
is reading sentences I know too well…
I've daydreamed through my host's long, windy praise!
It's time to put my Earthbound dream to work
and feed the hungry *and* the nibbling minds.
This brief applause lasts one deep breath, and lifts
me from my chair—and school is open here.

The Secret Pond

Oh, to steal away to the secret pond
that hides among high hills and, poised between
two watersheds, reflects a land beyond
the boundaries a world for sale has seen—

That liquid calm I reach alone on foot,
though trailhead crows might fly out north-northwest
to find the goal of an unmarked, winding route
which solitary wanderers know best.

I make the journey for no greater reason
than to search still waters with blue damselflies,
to follow swooping swallows in their season,
to be surprised by begging screech-owl cries.

Such small but ageless acts most count as naught
are holy things, if holy things there be;
the prize all kings have vainly sought, these caught
and kept in Nature's immortality.

It's mirrored now, and with it for a while
my own reflected form, still, as I pore
upon a living jewel of ancient style
that grants a further view I've traveled for:

Each time I reach this pond and drop the weight
of weathered pack, I feel the quiet change
and know the place is right to contemplate
the long path here and higher western range.

Organic Matter

Handfuls of earth I carry here
were maple leaves I raked last year.
New-made by worms (with no machines
in sight), this soil lacks only means
to shape it for some other use
than feeding maples, ash, or spruce.
The worms, I'm sure, will never miss
the traces that I take from this
to fertilize asparagus
since—just between the pair of us—
I give them back the bottom parts
and save my culinary arts
for tender tips. As for the trees—
what's made from seasoned leaves may please
or not; but there will likely fall
enough for worms, cooks, gardeners, all
to gather what they need, and then
transform that with their craft again.

About the Author and the Illustrator

New Paltz poet Roger Roloff, formerly an opera and concert baritone specializing in works by Wagner and Richard Strauss, has enjoyed writing in traditional and original verse forms for many years. When not working on a poem he may be found—depending on the season and often in the good company of his wife, Barbara—tending vegetable and flower gardens, berrying at home and in the wild, building firewood cords, or watching nature attentively from a study window or on hikes in the Shongum and Catskill Mountains. *The Poetry of Earth* is his second volume of poems.

Environmental educator Ilka List was introduced to Shawangunk Mountain paths in 1980 and continues to explore them with her wonderful friends and her dog. Ilka holds a Master's degree in Sculpture, a Doctorate in Art and Art Professions, and has written and illustrated several natural history books for children. In 1999 she developed a "therapeutic" garden as an additional setting for her practice as a psychotherapist. She conducts workshops in storytelling and nature as well, and loves visiting her children and grandchildren.